BRASS INSTRUMENTS

by
John Wood

BEARPORT
PUBLISHING

Minneapolis, Minnesota

Credits
All images are courtesy of Shutterstock.com, unless otherwise specified. With thanks to Getty Images, Thinkstock Photo, and iStockphoto. Recurring – paw, Visual Unit, Trikona. Cover – Quang Vinh Tran, StockSmartStart, H.Elvin, Vec.Stock. Page 2–3 – stockphoto-graf. Page 4–5 – alexandre zveiger, De Visu. Page 6–7 – Chromakey, Hep Town, CC BY 3.0 <https://creativecommons.org/licenses/by/3.0>, via Wikimedia Commons. Page 8–9 – goldpierre, Roland Godefroy, CC BY 3.0 <https://creativecommons.org/licenses/by/3.0>, via Wikimedia Commons. Page 10–11 – the palms, Matthias G. Ziegler. Page 12–13 – Boris Medvedev, Loco Steve. Page 14–15 – ANGHI. Page 16–17 – furtseff, Zachi Evenor, CC BY-SA 4.0 <https://creativecommons.org/licenses/by-sa/4.0>, via Wikimedia Commons. Page 18–19 – sirtravelalot, SeventyFour. Page 20–21 – The Swedish History Museum, Stockholm from Sweden, CC BY 2.0 <https://creativecommons.org/licenses/by/2.0>, via Wikimedia Commons, Maria-Kitaeva, Andrew Glushchenko, Afrumgartz. Page 22–23 – De Visu, James Kirkikis, joseph s l tan matt, Igor Bulgarin.

Bearport Publishing Company Product Development Team
President: Jen Jenson; Director of Product Development: Spencer Brinker; Managing Editor: Allison Juda; Associate Editor: Naomi Reich; Associate Editor: Tiana Tran; Art Director: Colin O'Dea; Designer: Kim Jones; Designer: Kayla Eggert; Product Development Assistant: Owen Hamlin

Library of Congress Cataloging-in-Publication Data

Names: Wood, John, 1990- author.
Title: Brass instruments / by John Wood.
Description: Fusion books. | Minneapolis, Minnesota : Bearport Publishing
    Company, 2024. | Series: All about instruments | Includes index.
Identifiers: LCCN 2023059726 (print) | LCCN 2023059727 (ebook) | ISBN
    9798889169666 (library binding) | ISBN 9798892324762 (paperback) | ISBN
    9798892321129 (ebook)
Subjects: LCSH: Brass instruments--Juvenile literature.
Classification: LCC ML933 .W66 2024 (print) | LCC ML933 (ebook)
LC record available at https://lccn.loc.gov/2023059726
LC ebook record available at https://lccn.loc.gov/2023059727

© 2025 BookLife Publishing
This edition is published by arrangement with BookLife Publishing.

North American adaptations © 2025 Bearport Publishing Company. All rights reserved. No part of this publication may be reproduced in whole or in part, stored in any retrieval system, or transmitted in any form or by any means, electronic, mechanical, photocopying, recording, or otherwise, without written permission from the publisher. Bearport Publishing is a division of Chrysalis Education Group.

For more information, write to Bearport Publishing, 5357 Penn Avenue South, Minneapolis, MN 55419.

CONTENTS

Join the Band. 4
Instruments from History 6
Making Sound with Brass. 8
Shofar. 10
French Horn 11
Trombone 12
Trumpet. 14
Flugelhorn 16
Tuba. 17
Sousaphone 18
Euphonium 20
Bugle 21
What Will You Play? 22
Glossary 24
Index 24

JOIN THE BAND

Do you love music? Have you ever wanted to play an instrument? Let's join a band!

This book is about brass instruments. Today, these instruments are often made of brass or other metals. But humans have been playing instruments for much longer than brass has been around.

Musicians in a band often play different instruments.

Instruments from History

People played flutes made of bone tens of thousands of years ago.

ABOUT 4,500 YEARS AGO

40,000 YEARS AGO

Lyres are some of the oldest string instruments in the world.

MAKING SOUND WITH BRASS

Today, brass instruments are very popular. They are all played in a similar way. Musicians buzz their lips into the **mouthpiece**, which makes air **vibrate** through the instrument.

You hear the vibrations from brass instruments as sound.

The length of the **tubing** in an instrument changes the **pitch**, or how high and low a sound is. Longer tubes make lower pitches. Shorter tubes mean higher pitches. **Slides** and **valves** can change the length of tubing.

SLIDE

Pressing a valve or moving a slide opens up longer paths of tubing.

FRENCH HORN

The French horn is a little more modern. But it has changed over time. Players used to make different pitches by sticking their hand into the bell. Now, most French horns have valves moved by levers.

LEVERS

BELL

If a French horn were rolled out, it would be almost 18 feet (5 m) long.

TROMBONE

A trombone is a big brass instrument. It has a slide that is pushed and pulled to make different **notes**.

BELL

SLIDE

MOUTHPIECE

The trombone can make sounds with a low pitch.

12

Gunhild Carling is a musician who plays many instruments, including the trombone. She travels around the world with her family's band.

Gunhild knows how to play more than 10 instruments.

GUNHILD CARLING

TRUMPET

The trumpet is a small but loud brass instrument. It has three valves.

The trumpet has a finger hook to help you hold it.

FINGER HOOK

VALVE

14

Dizzy Gillespie was a famous jazz trumpet player. He was known for puffing his cheeks out when he played.

DIZZY GILLESPIE

Dizzy Gillespie played a trumpet that pointed upward.

Dizzy helped create a new musical style called bebop.

FLUGELHORN

A flugelhorn (floo-guhl-HORN) has three valves. Players make different notes by pressing down different valves. This instrument sounds a bit like a trumpet but softer.

The flugelhorn was invented in Austria in the 1830s.

BELL

VALVE

TUBA

The tuba is a huge, heavy brass instrument. It makes a deep, low-pitched sound. To play a tuba, you hold it so the bell points upward.

BELL

MOUTHPIECE

VALVE

There are some giant tubas that are bigger than a person!

SOUSAPHONE

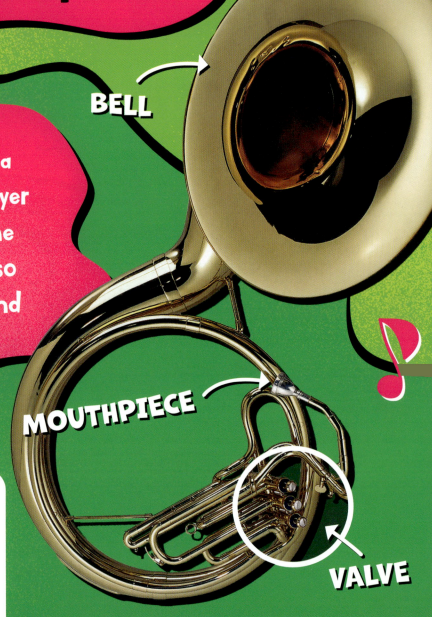

BELL

MOUTHPIECE

VALVE

A sousaphone (SOO-zuh-fone) is a lot like a tuba. A player puts the sousaphone around their body so they can walk around while they play.

The sousaphone was invented in the United States in the late 1800s.

FLAMING TUBA

There are lots of weird brass instruments that people make themselves. Have you heard of the **flaming** sousaphone or the flaming tuba?

These instruments can shoot out fire while they are being played.

EUPHONIUM

BELL

A euphonium (yoo-**FOH**-nee-uhm) looks like a small tuba. Like many other brass instruments, it has a water key. This part opens up to let out spit that has gathered in the instrument!

Euphoniums sometimes have three valves and sometimes have four.

WATER KEY

BUGLE

Bugle calls were used to send messages across battlefields or while hunting.

Bugles are small and usually made out of brass or copper. They have no valves or slides, which means they can only play a few notes. Different patterns of notes are known as calls.

TUBING

MOUTHPIECE

WHAT WILL YOU PLAY?

Now you know all about brass instruments! Pick your instrument and join a band.

Jazz bands have trumpets and flugelhorns.

Brass bands and **marching bands** are full of trumpets, trombones, and sousaphones.

Mariachi is a type of music from Mexico that uses trumpets.

Many brass instruments play in classical music bands. They often have loud, powerful parts.

It is time to start playing!

Glossary

flaming being on fire

marching bands groups of musicians who play instruments while marching

mouthpiece the part of an instrument where you place your mouth to play

musicians people who make or play music

notes musical sounds of a certain pitch that last for a length of time

pitch the highness or lowness of a sound

slides U-shaped parts of instruments that can be moved to make different sounds

tubing the hollow part of an instrument between the mouthpiece and the open end

valves devices that control the flow of air in an instrument, making the sound higher or lower

vibrate to move back and forth very quickly

Index

bands 4–5, 13, 22–23
bell 11–12, 16–18, 20
Carling, Gunhild 13
flaming tuba 19
metals 5
Gillespie, Dizzy 15
mouthpiece 8, 12, 17–18, 21
pitch 9, 11–12, 17
slides 9, 12, 21
valves 9, 11, 14, 16, 20–21
vibrations 8